# Restoring
# Fellowship

# Restoring Fellowship

by
## Joy P. Gage
and
## Kenneth G. Gage

**MOODY PRESS**

CHICAGO

For
The Salt Company—
the class
with whom we first shared
these ideas

©1984 by
THE MOODY BIBLE INSTITUTE
OF CHICAGO

**Library of Congress Cataloging in Publication Data**

Gage, Joy P.
    Restoring fellowship.

    1. Church discipline.    I. Gage, Kenneth G.,
1928-      . II. Title.
BV650.2.G34    1984              262.9                    84-14700
ISBN 0-8024-4440-7 (pbk.)

        1  2  3  4  5  6  7  Printing/BC/Year 88  87  86  85  84

*Printed in the United States of America*

# Contents

70747

# Foreword

You could say that Joy and Kenneth Gage have written a book about surgery: spiritual surgery. The point is simple. The individual Christian and the congregation to which he belongs are in constant need of the loving and skillful hand of the spiritual surgeon who spots the "cancer" of sin and chooses to do something about it.

The congregation is not a place free of sin's cancer and its consequences. In fact sometimes one gets the impression that sin is more apparent within than without. Perhaps that is because a healthy congregation is not afraid to talk about issues that lie hidden in the heart and among relationships—not only to talk but to do something about them. Beyond the congregation, out in the "real world," there is a tendency to ignore the roots of sin and to rationalize its consequences.

But the Bible simply will not permit the follower of Jesus Christ to do that, whether it be in the realm of personal behavior or the conduct of intercongregational relationships. God set a garden in order with certain rules; He gave Israel a series of laws by which to live. He sent prophets to confront people who broke them; He gave priests to create conditions for forgiveness and restoration. The pages of the New Testament are filled with reminders to pursue holiness and to deal firmly and swiftly with things that threaten the vitality of the life of the Christian or the Christian community. And all of that has something to do with what we call discipline.

Today the contemporary church struggles with the subject of discipline. It is not popular to judge one another, nor is it an easy thing to confront one another. Many would rather ignore sin and conflict than go through the struggle of facing it and forgiving it under proper conditions. But we cannot hope for an effective ministry in the 1980s and 90s and neglect the necessary purification of our lives and of our fellowship.

As in older times, trusted brothers and sisters frequently fall in spiritual warfare as soldiers do in military warfare. Honorable people find themselves on different sides of the fence in a dispute. A new Christian brings the "excess baggage" of behavior patterns into the church, some of which are simply intolerable to the life-style of the believing community. Partners sharing business interests slowly discover that their ambitions, their strategies, or their systems of work put them on divergent paths. A marriage relationship goes awry because of errors in judgment or failure to maintain the relationship.

All of these and many other scenarios are the stuff of personal performance and conflict that can destroy people, reputations, and relationships if not properly dealt with. The apostle Paul knew that, and that is why he wrote to the Philippian congregation and pleaded with them to work hard at bringing together two women who were in dispute. He knew that if the congregation did not enter into disciplinary exercise over the women, everyone would soon be caught up in their struggle. As in those days, there must be today those in the church who are exhorters, confronters, healers, and peacemakers. And that is what this book is about.

Confronting and peacemaking are the major concerns of Joy and Kenneth Gage. They have chosen to write about the most difficult part. Their instructions as to how to expose conflict, ungodly behavior, and destructive choices will help the pastor and the lay leader who are in great need of insight and resolve. While they understand compassion, they also appreciate the need for firmness. And while they urge affection, they also point out to us that sometimes there is a bit of pain involved in the surgery that the spiritual body requires. We need to be reminded of these things today.

As our Western world lapses more and more into an un-Christian perspective, and as human behavior is increasingly gauged by pagan standards, it will become necessary for Christian leaders to raise the standard of holiness and Christian discipline higher. For to rationalize sin and not confront it will be to sow the seeds of ultimate destruction for congregations. Joy and Kenneth Gage have provided an excellent primer on this subject. Their insights fit the times in which we live. Now may God grant each of us the courage to implement the things they bring to our attention.

GORDON MACDONALD
Pastor, Grace Chapel
Lexington, Massachusetts

# A Pastor's Dilemma

Of all the responsibilities of the pastor, the most painful surely must be the responsibility to lead the church in disciplinary action.

I had not been a minister very long before I was faced with this unpleasant task. The ordeal was made tolerable only by the fact that pastor and board were united in the action. In that church we faced several additional discipline cases. But the church remained a strong influence in the community as we handled each incident in a scriptural manner.

Friends in the ministry have faced similar problems— some much more serious. Some have even been called upon to discipline a fellow pastor. Somehow the necessity of the action never lessens the pain of those who must participate in the discipline.

The issue of church discipline is often complicated because of widespread confusion about what the Bible says on the subject of judging. Many believers are sincerely troubled over the question, Are we ever supposed to judge another believer?

Others may concur that when a member of the body is found to be in open sin, something must be done. Something—but what? Very few have carefully thought through their position on what the church should do when confronted with the problem. Perhaps the unspoken assumption (and secret hope) is that when some carnal member falls into gross sin, he will immediately go away. Then the church will not have to initiate any action.

Strange thing about sin within the body—it is hardly ever restricted to a carnal member whose attendance is infrequent at best. Perhaps that is part of the confusion. We are easily incensed by immoral actions of a total stranger. We hear about them on television or read about them in the morning paper, and we are instantly repelled. Yet when we learn of the same action perpetrated by a close friend, the immediate reaction is seldom one of repulsion. Instead it is apt to be "God, don't let this be true!"

At such times, the most carefully thought out theory seems totally inadequate. In fact, theories have a way of going out the window when the one in need of discipline is everyone's best friend, or favorite Sunday school teacher, or the star of the church bowling team.

There came a time when I was faced with such a case. From the onset I realized that it was different from all past cases. Emotions ran high. Confusion was everywhere evident. I found myself walking the floor night after night seeking God's answer to man's sin.

I was unprepared for the conflicting feelings verbalized by the congregation and for the division that developed. I was unprepared for some of the implications of the case that resulted from our judicial system. I was unprepared to make some of the decisions I was called upon to make.

It was a painful, heartrending experience that raised many questions. Out of the experience came a determination to discover the whole counsel of God regarding judging.

My wife shared my determination. Together we began a study of all the New Testament passages on the topic.

We discovered that church discipline is but one part of the total subject. It is quite clear that judging does not always involve condemnation and/or censure. There are at least four major categories of judging covered in the Scriptures: condemnation (censure), arbitration, critical evaluation, and discernment.

Perhaps our most important discovery concerned the consequences of faulty judgment (failure to judge, judging all the wrong things, inability to make good judgments). There are serious consequences for both the individual believer and the local church body. Although those consequences are highly visible (weak believers, weak and carnal churches) they are rarely attributed to a judgment problem.

We believe it is time to cut through the confusion about judging. We believe that a proper understanding of the biblical concept of judging will lead to stronger Christians and stronger churches. Thus, some three years later, we offer this treatise.

It is our prayer that through these pages you will discover some answers to the question, "What does the Bible say about judging and making judgments?" In turn, may that discovery equip you to discern personal responsibility in matters of judging.

KENNETH G. GAGE

# 1

## To Judge or Not to Judge

To judge or not to judge has long been the question. The church had hardly forgotten its birthpangs before it became necessary for apostolic leaders to deal with the question of judging. There was confusion then. There is confusion now.

"Are Christians ever supposed to judge?" "Isn't all judging wrong?" "Aren't we supposed to forgive instead of throwing stones?"

Ask any group of Christians what they know about judging, and, without a doubt, the most common answer will be "Judge not that ye be not judged." Many believers assume that passage (Matthew 7:1) is all that the Bible teaches on the subject. They conclude that they must never make a value judgment on what is right or wrong for another Christian.

The question "We're never supposed to judge, are we?" will usually arise during times of gross immorality within the local church. That is not to say that the one posing the

question condones the immorality. Rather, he assumes he
must effect a "see no evil, hear no evil, speak no evil"
attitude even though he is personally incensed over another believer's sin.

Greg was the minister of music in a large church. One
Sunday night after the service he walked into the senior
minister's office and turned in his keys and his letter of
resignation. He gave no explanation for his action. "You'll
know soon enough," he said, and walked out.

On Monday morning, Greg moved to a distant city, taking with him the wife of one of the church elders. Two
marriages were broken. Several children were involved.

By the following Sunday everyone had heard the news.
In the rehearsal room, twenty-five somber-faced choir
members donned their robes in preparation for the morning worship service. Most of them felt angry, shocked, and
personally betrayed. But only one dared voice her feelings.

After making sure that no one else could hear her, she
blurted out to the substitute director, "I'm so upset by what
Greg did. But that's wrong, isn't it? I mean the Bible says
we're never supposed to judge, doesn't it?"

Her confusion is typical.

When sin suddenly invades the body, the members experience a series of reactions. "It can't be true!" "How
could he do this to us?" "I feel guilty about judging, but I
can't help it."

Because the uninformed believer concludes that all judging is wrong, he feels guilty every time he forms an opinion
about another believer's plunge into immorality. He becomes increasingly frustrated because he cannot deal with
his conflicting feelings. "I'm so angry at him. But I'm not
supposed to judge!" Often he angrily verbalizes his frus-
tration by demanding that the minister or board "do something about this."

The fact is, a believer cannot go through life without
judging and making judgments. Nor is he expected to do
so. Just as surely as the Bible commands believers to refrain

from judging in certain situations, so it requires believers to judge in others. Confusion can only be dispelled by familiarizing oneself with all the Scriptures that pertain to the subject.

In our study we discovered that the New Testament has over 200 references to judging and making judgments. Based on three Greek root forms, those references are variously translated: judge, examine, condemn, discern. Of those references, almost one fourth occur in the book of 1 Corinthians.

In addition, we discovered that 1 Corinthians is characterized by the use of a literary device known as the rhetorical question. The apostle Paul uses this device approximately seventy-five times in 1 Corinthians, more than in all his other writings combined. He asks seventy-five questions which, although they do not call for a vocal response, call for a mental conclusion—a judgment.

These discoveries prompted us to use 1 Corinthians as the basic text for this study. It is probably the most comprehensive passage of Scripture on the subject of judging. It addresses many questions. What should be judged? What should not be judged? Why should we judge? Who should judge? What formula should be followed?

In fact, 1 Corinthians is a manual on the subject. One could subtitle the book "All you ever wanted to know about judging, but didn't know where to look."

Dispelling confusion about any biblical question begins with correct Bible study techniques. Answers are not to be found in isolated verses. Answers can only be found as the student examines the big picture. What other passages relate to the subject? What is the context of the verses being considered?

Seeing a piece of literature (in this case a Bible book) as a whole is of utmost importance. If the reader can pick up the author's theme and think his thoughts with him as he moves through his material, then the reader will comprehend the details within the whole.

This we have endeavored to do. We have tried to think through the whole in order to focus on the details. We have attempted to discover the conclusions of the author in order to apply them to the twentieth-century church.

One thing is immediately evident. The Corinthians were guilty of two errors in judging. They judged all the wrong things, and they failed to judge that which should have been judged. In each case Paul pointed to the relationship of pride to their problem.

We will examine that relationship in the following chapter.

# 2

# Pride, Prejudice, and Party Spirit

Pride, disunity, and faulty judging are all issues central to the theme of 1 Corinthians. In fact, as we outlined the book we found it difficult to determine the main issue. Our conclusion is that the three issues are interrelated. In the case of the Corinthian church, one problem could not be eliminated apart from the others.

Pride permeated their lives, and thus the life of the church. Their pride of identity led them to judge spiritual leaders. Pride in their tolerance of sin kept them from judging it within the church body. Pride in spiritual gifts led them to seek the showiest gifts, oblivious to the fact that the Holy Spirit distributes gifts as He will for the edification of the Body as a whole. Pride in their possessions and station caused them to neglect and disdain (a form of judging) believers who had neither.

But most important to the subject of this book is the fact that pride affected their ability to judge or to withhold judgment in a proper manner.

*How pride affects judging.* If one would grasp the scriptural dos and don'ts of judging, one must first understand how pride colors any act of judging. Two well-known quotations illustrate this fact.

"God, I thank thee that I am not as. . .this publican" (Luke 18:11).

"There, but for the grace of God goes John Bradford."[1]

In each case the speaker has made a value judgment regarding another man. But the presence of pride changes the entire character of an otherwise neutral assessment of someone's need.

Assessing another's need normally involves making a judgment. In itself, the act is neither right nor wrong. It is simply a statement based on an assessment of known facts.

Believers make such judgments almost daily. Many times they are made within a positive context. "My neighbor is an alcoholic. Pray for him and for me that I may be a help to him and to his family."

When pride enters in, the neutral act has a negative connotation. "God, I thank you I am not like this man!" Such an attitude indicates that the speaker is oblivious to the grace of God in his own life. It also indicates a lack of response to another's needs. Certainly it diminishes one's ability to minister to the needy individual.

Pride becomes the deciding factor in otherwise neutral acts of judging. Thus, on the list "Dos and Don'ts of Judging," number one should be "Never judge out of pride."

*Pride divides the body.* The consequences of pride may be seen as one examines the Corinthians' attitude toward spiritual leaders. What appears to be a matter of preference is actually a problem of pride; in this case, a pride of identity.

It is evident that the Corinthians had personal preferences among those who had ministered to them. It is also

1. Attributed to John Bradford (1510?-1555) in *Five Thousand Quotations for All Occasions*, ed. Lewis C. Henry (Garden City, N.Y.: Doubleday, Garden City, 1952), p. 112.

evident that they criticized those not preferred. Their criticism is seen to be a form of judging. They were critical of Paul's preaching. They were also critical of his ministry as a whole.

Paul responded to their criticism by defending both his ministry and his message. He declared that God was the one who determined the message of the apostles. He explained rather bluntly that the scope of the message was limited by the spiritual immaturity of the listeners. In this case those listeners were his critics.

He defended his ministry as a whole by declaring, "It is a small thing I am judged of you. My conscience is clear but that isn't what makes me acceptable to God. God is the real judge and in His own time He will judge every man's work" (1 Corinthians 4:3-4).

Are we to assume by these statements that as believers we dare not have any preference among spiritual leaders? Hardly. Such an idealistic goal denies the fact that man is a highly individual creature. People are different. Spiritual leaders are different. People relate differently.

Should we assume that we must never judge the content of a spiritual leader's message? Certainly not. Surely such an assumption is dangerous as well as unscriptural.

Paul himself commanded the Corinthians to judge what he said. The Christians at Berea were commended because they searched the Scriptures daily for the specific purpose of judging what the apostle taught. It is a practice believers should follow today.

The key to the Corinthian problem may be found in the statements "I am of Paul" and "I am of Apollos." Even in English it should be obvious that the Corinthian believer was not saying that Paul or Apollos was great. Rather, he was saying, "I am great because I am identified with Paul (or Apollos)!"

The Greek clarifies it even further. "I" is a double "I." The emphasis is not on the preferred apostle. Although the distinction between preference of leaders and pride of

identity may seem small, it is an important key to interpretation. Pride spells the difference between unity and
disunity. Pride of identity divides the Body of Christ. In
the very act of assuming pride through identity one is
placed in the position of judging those who are not of the
same identity.

*Pride and the "perfect" church.* To understand the significance of the pride problem, consider for a moment the
qualifications of an ideal church. How would you picture
it? Would such a church include a group of believers who
are growing in their knowledge of the Word, boldly witnessing, exercising spiritual gifts, and eagerly awaiting the
Lord's return? Those are wonderful, positive characteristics. What more could one ask in a church?

Does it surprise you that the Corinthian church had all
these (see 1 Corinthians 1:4-7). Yet down through the centuries this church has always been seen as a negative example. Why?

In spite of their knowledge of the Word, in spite of their
zeal, in spite of their spiritual gifts, in spite of the fact that
they were looking for the Lord's return, Paul labeled the
Corinthian body a carnal church.

He pointed to the source of their carnality—"One says
'I am of Paul' and another 'I am of Apollos.'" He pointed
to the consequences—"You are too immature to receive
deeper truths. I can only give you basics!" Their carnality
impeded the development of spiritual maturity (1 Corinthians 3:1-4).

Problems with pride are just as prevalent today as in the
first-century church. Pride of identity is evident everywhere—identity with people because of who they are or
what they have; identity with labels; identity through clubs;
identity through status symbols; and yes, identity with great
Bible teachers.

Such things are neutral in themselves. They are neither
good nor bad. Neither position nor possession should be
looked upon as evil. But when the possession or the po-

sition leads to an exaggerated pride of identity, the result is the same today as with the Corinthian church. Pride divides the Body, deters spiritual growth, distorts judgment, and defends sin.

There are serious implications in this picture for the church in general and the individual believer in particular. Pride begins in the heart of the individual. Unchecked, it can quickly become a corporate problem that affects the spiritual life of the entire body.

Because pride is an attitude, it is primarily a problem that must be solved on a personal level. If your church does not seem to measure up these days, perhaps it is time to take a spiritual inventory. Make sure that you are part of the solution—not at the heart of the problem.

# DIVISION I:

# JUDGING THAT INVOLVES
# CONDEMNATION OR CENSURE

Of those Greek roots that translate to some variation of "judge" or "making judgments," *krino* is the most frequently used.

In the Greek New Testament there are at least twenty-two words that are derived from the root, *krino*.

It is the root *krino* that normally appears wherever condemnation or censure is indicated.

To censure or condemn another human being is a serious action. Since the Bible both commands this practice and forbids it, it is essential to discover the limitations and qualifications that go with the directives.

In the following three chapters we will examine three familiar passages: 1 Corinthians 5, Matthew 7:1, and James 4:11-12. In the first passage the corporate body is directed to censure a sinning brother. In the latter passages believers are forbidden to judge.

# 3

# The Church's Responsibility to Judge Sin
### (1 Corinthians 5)

"Who are we to throw stones?" "What he does is between him and God." "This is not our responsibility."

One can well imagine the Corinthian grapevine regarding the believer who had become involved in an illicit relationship.

Much can be assumed about the Corinthians from the opening verses of chapter 5. They were the original broad-minded Christians. They closed their eyes to another man's sin. They looked the other way. Perhaps they were proud of their ability to accept a brother no matter what he did— proud of an open fellowship, which excluded no one who claimed to belong to Jesus Christ.

How they actually verbalized their pride and tolerance must be left to the imagination; however, it is obvious that they had a basic problem with attitude. Paul clearly stated that they were proud when they should have been mourning over the man's sin.

*The church charged with censuring its own.* Paul demanded

that the church take immediate action to correct the situation. He charged the church with the responsibility to censure the guilty believer.

It is important to note that the command to judge this believer was given to the church as a body. The censure was to be a corporate (not an individual) action.

It is also important to see that neither personal conviction nor corporate consensus determined the man's guilt. His guilt was determined by uncontestable evidence that he was practicing sexual misconduct clearly forbidden by God.

It was public knowledge that the man was sleeping with his father's wife. Such conduct was socially unacceptable even in the amoral society of the pagan community. The nature of the sin and the extent to which it was known necessitated discipline by the body.

In addition to pointing out the necessity for censure and the church's corporate responsibility in the matter, Paul also explained the purpose and the procedure.

*The purpose of censure* (vv. 1,5,6-8). There was a threefold purpose for the censure. First (and this is implied) the judging was for the sake of the community. It is well to remember that a church loses its witness not so much through the sin of a member as through the lack of corporate judgment upon that sin. In failing to judge sin in the church, the church becomes open to judgment by the world. A corrupt church has little to offer a corrupt world.

Second, the judgment was for the sake of the individual. This is not a punitive judgment. This judgment was to serve as a corrective, disciplinary measure. Such discipline was necessary in order that the believer might repent, cease from his sin, and be restored to fellowship.

Verse 5 indicates that the purpose of the censure was to accomplish something of spiritual value within the sinning believer's life.

Third, the judgment was for the sake of the church. Tolerating sin within the body corrupts the entire body (vv. 6-8). Paul told them it was necessary to exclude the guilty believer in order to cleanse the body.

*The procedure.* The actual procedure may seem obscure, but it is clear that the censure involved an exclusion from the fellowship. Five times in this chapter Paul refers to an act of exclusion (vv. 2,5,7,11,13).

This passage includes several obscure statements that theologians debate.

1. "Deliver such a one to Satan." Verse 5 is something of a theological "fuzzy." That is to say, its obscurity captures the imagination of the theologian. The tendency is to major on that which is fuzzy while ignoring that which is clear. It is of course more intellectually stimulating to crack the obscure than to pursue the obvious.

Concerning oneself with the obscure raises such questions as "What does it mean to deliver one to Satan?" "What is the exact process?" "How will the flesh be destroyed?" The passage is discussed, debated, explained, and expounded.

Our conclusion is that when the believer who has sinned is excluded from the protective fellowship of the body, he is then exposed to all the wiles and wrath of Satan. The hedge is removed. He is in a vulnerable position.

There are those who concur with this position, but whether or not we come to a theological consensus on the interpretation of this phrase is of minor importance.

There are some very obvious facts in this passage. It is obvious that the church was to exclude the man. It is obvious that the purpose of this exclusion was to accomplish something of a spiritual value in the man's life. Further, we believe we may safely assume that the Body of Christ is neither in the business of destroying flesh nor of saving spirits. It should be obvious that this process is under God's jurisdiction. Although Satan is indicated as one who will destroy the flesh, even this is under God's jurisdiction. (Satan was restricted from taking Job's life, Job 2:1-6.)

From these obvious facts we conclude that the severe disciplinary action is actually in God's hand. The responsibility of the church is to censure the individual by excluding him from fellowship.

This being the case it would also appear that the failure of the church to take the responsibility of excluding the individual could actually hinder any restorative work that God desires to initiate. How can one face the awfulness of his sin so long as he enjoys the comforting fellowship of God's people?

2. "With such a man do not eat." Theologians also debate the correct interpretation of verse 11. In our opinion, the better interpretation calls for excluding the guilty man from the Lord's Table. This opinion is based chiefly on our understanding of the context.

Observe that after commanding the Corinthians to "deliver such a one to Satan" Paul refers again to their attitude (compare verses 2 and 6). He then digresses into a lecture on leaven and the feast, noting that a little leaven leavens the whole lump. He commands them to purge out the old lump because Christ our Passover Lamb is sacrificed for us. He urges them to keep the feast without the old leaven and without malice and wickedness.

Jewish custom demanded purging the house of leaven at the time of the Passover feast. This was a symbolic cleansing required by the law in preparation for the festal celebration.

Christ changed the significance of this feast for His followers at the time of His last Passover supper with His disciples. He said, "This is My body which is broken, My blood which is shed for you. This do in remembrance of Me." From that day the disciples kept the feast not in remembrance of the deliverance of Israel from Egypt, but in remembrance of the world's deliverance from sin through Christ, the true Passover Lamb. Such was the custom of the early church.

The new feast was not subject to the laws surrounding the Jewish Passover. But as Paul here points out, cleansing was a necessary part of the new feast just as it had been of the old.

The apostle next acknowledges there is no way one can avoid contact with people who practice immorality, extortion, idolatry, or coveting so long as one is in this world. But he commands them to exclude from their midst anyone who calls himself a brother and is practicing certain sins. In addition to immorality he specifically cites the problems of greed, idolatry, abusive tongues, drunkenness, and extortion. "With such people (who claim to be Christians)," he commanded, "do not eat." He concludes the entire chapter by once again admonishing the church, "Put out that wicked person from your midst."

The weight of the context points to an act of exclusion from the Communion table; however there are those who favor a more literal interpretation of verse 11 as it stands alone. In the Living Bible, Kenneth Taylor renders the phrase, "Don't even eat lunch." Paul E. Engle, in an article in *Moody Monthly* (May 1981), also favors this interpretation. He specifically mentions "no more spontaneous invitations for strawberry shortcake after a church service. No more pizza parties with Christian friends at a local restaurant. No more sharing mutual joys and concerns over coffee."

If the apostle is indeed saying "don't eat lunch" (or pizza or dessert) with the disciplined individual, one must still raise the question of exclusion from the Communion table. It would hardly seem consistent to partake of Communion with someone with whom one would refuse to have lunch.

The chief difference to be reconciled between the two interpretations is the question of responsibility in censuring. In verses 2, 4, and 13 Paul places responsibility upon the church as a body for corporate action in censuring the man who was guilty of sexual sin. If in verse 11 he is indeed saying that one must not even eat lunch with a believer who is guilty of certain sins, then the act of judging becomes an individual responsibility as well as a corporate one.

In our research we have failed to find a single passage in which the individual believer is to initiate an act of condemnation or censure on a one-to-one basis. This type of judging seems to be reserved for the corporate body.

"What then is the responsibility of the individual believer

toward the censured brother?" one might ask.

It is reasonable to assume that the intent of the corporate discipline must be supported by the members. Close friends of the censured brother will find it necessary to make some adjustment in the relationship. Although love and/or concern may be expressed, it must be tempered by a refusal to condone the censured action.

If this seems hard, bear in mind that the purpose of the censure is restorative, not punitive. One does not accomplish restoration through unbroken fellowship where everything proceeds as if nothing had happened.

The purpose of an act of censure can be effectively counteracted if well-meaning but unwise friends surround the brother with loving acceptance.

Whatever interpretation one takes for verse 5 or 11, the act of censure by exclusion cannot be missed. In the closing verses of the chapter Paul uses the term *judging* three times with reference to excluding from fellowship those who are guilty of specific sins. He emphasizes that we have no responsibility to judge unbelievers. Only God does that. But we must judge believers—by exclusion.

Lest the principle be applied too broadly, it is well to review the facts.

(1) The sin to be censured in this passage was a sin of incest, which was publicly known and condemned even by Gentile society. (2) It was to be judged by the corporate body. (3) The judgment consisted of an act of exclusion. (4) The purpose of the action was to initiate a process by which the sinning brother would be restored to fellowship with God and the church. The action was also intended as a purifying measure for the church.

It should be clear that the church does have a responsibility to censure its own.

This brings us to the question, How can the body apply scriptural discipline in the twentieth century, and what problems may be anticipated?

# 4

# Can Scriptural Discipline Be Administered by the Twentieth-Century Church?

"How is the act of exclusion accomplished today?" one might ask. "With great difficulty!" the experienced pastor would reply.

A variety of problems are encountered by the twentieth-century church that dares to discipline. Not the least of those problems is found in the area of structure. It is one thing to exclude an individual from a first-century fellowship of believers. It is quite another to exclude one from a twentieth-century public worship service.

Because of the very public nature of most functions of the contemporary church, exclusion is not easily accomplished. If exclusion is the aim of the discipline, then the question of attendance must be considered along with the questions of membership and responsibilities within the church.

*Case history A.* Consider for example this contemporary case history. In a large western city a faithful member of an evangelical congregation became involved in immoral-

ity. When it was openly known, the church took official
action. He was stripped of membership and of all official
duties. Technically he was cut off from official fellowship.
But practically speaking the discipline accomplished very
little other than to take away his voting privileges and his
right to serve. He continued to attend the worship service,
which was open to the public. He even partook of Communion, which was served to visitors as well as to members.

Some members were offended. Some were quite angry.
Most were confused. A few left. Eventually the minister
and several elders went to the man and explained that he
was not welcome as long as he continued in his sin.

This case illustrates a basic weakness in the most popular
formula for church discipline. To strip the sinning believer
of all duties and/or membership (in some churches membership is dropped as a secondary measure) has long been
considered the best way to handle discipline cases. The
congregation either participates in the action or is informed of it.

Problems are seldom solved by this formula. But they
often go away. Many times the result of the action is that
the disciplined member disappears, never to be seen again.
In effect, an act of exclusion seems to have taken place. In
reality, the exclusion is at the volition of the censured member.

Because this happens so often, little thought is given to
the scope of the discipline. No one asks, "Should he be
allowed to worship with us?" because it is assumed he will
not want to do so. No one presses for dropping his name
from the rolls because it is assumed that a censured member will never have the nerve to come to a business meeting
and cast his vote. In the vast majority of cases those as-
sumptions are correct. But it is well to remember that nothing in the church action dictates the exclusion.

Certainly in a day when the right of the individual is
being championed there can be complications in any move
toward exclusion. To bar someone from attendance at a

public meeting might precipitate legal action. But the lack of total solutions should not discourage churches from exercising discipline. The worst possible solution is to avoid the discipline which is clearly needed. This should never be considered an option.

Discipline calls for strong leadership. The first action of that leadership (minister and board) should be to unite in prayer.

"Many people advised me what to do," writes one minister, "but not one deacon, not one person ever offered to pray with me or for me in the decisions we were facing."

Before any decision is made the leadership should spend time together on their knees. That leadership should also be united in thought. That is not to say they should cast votes until they come to an agreement on a course of action, but that together they should search the Scriptures to seek the correct biblical action.

Ideally the pastor should be able to lead them in this search. If the pastor is reluctant to "make waves" he may hesitate to initiate any action. This is no time to start an all-out campaign against the pastor's leadership—or lack of it. That would simply score another point for the enemy, who has already scored an impressive victory through the sinning believer. Instead, the occasion calls for persistent prodding to get together, search the Scriptures, and pray as a unit. It calls for open communication, mutual respect, and a determination to see the problem through together.

If after searching the Scripture together a decision cannot be reached, the best course of action is to return again as a group to prayer. When hearts are right before God and there is a sincere desire to know the will of God through His Word, unity will come.

*Case history B.* This case presents an example with both legal and theological implications.

A deacon in a congregationally governed church was arrested for a sexual act punishable by law. He was respected in his community and loved in his church. Initial reaction of Christian friends when reading the public account of his arrest was one of disbelief.

The minister went to the man, taking along two deacons. Ashamed and repentant, the man confessed his sin to the three and begged their forgiveness. They offered their support and forgiveness even as they spelled out the consequences. For the time being he was to be relieved of all his responsibilities in the church.

The man requested that his membership be dropped to avoid offending others; but he pleaded for permission to attend services in order to get his life back together. Permission was readily granted.

So far, so good? Not really.

At this point a legal problem entered the picture. Advised by his attorney to "say nothing, and change nothing about your life-style until a plea is entered," the defendant spoke in confidence to the pastor and deacons. Understandably he could make no move to publicly acknowledge his repentance. Nor could the pastor and deacons reveal what had been spoken in confidence.

The wheels of justice turn rather slowly, and with three intervening weeks before a plea was entered, great havoc was wrought in the church. Although the sin was a matter of public record, the confession and repentance were not.

Some members resented the fact that the man continued to worship with them as though nothing had happened. Others flew to his defense with "We're never supposed to judge!"

The minister tried to contain the situation by asking the congregation to be patient until such time as the plea was entered; but neither emotions nor opinions could be controlled.

The move proved to be detrimental to the congregation as a whole. Of equal importance is that it proved to be detrimental to the man himself.

There is something about playing out a role that quenches the work of the Holy Spirit within the heart of any individual. Three weeks is a long time to worship as if nothing had happened. Three weeks is a long time to withhold a public statement. Although initially repentant, the man became hard and defensive. In the end no public acknowledgement of repentance was made.

This case history might have been resolved in a more positive manner had it not been for the legal implications; however, there is a theological problem that also had a bearing on the case.

The pastor and deacons followed a pattern prescribed in Matthew 18:15-17. This passage calls for going to an individual on a one-to-one basis, then with two or three witnesses, and finally, if he refuses to listen, to the church.

Although the passage predates the church, there are those who make a strong case for applying it to matters of church discipline. Even those who argue that Matthew has little to say about church practice often accept this passage as a good formula for church discipline procedure.

The application is theologically incorrect. At issue in the Matthew passage is a private problem between two individuals. Church action is the final step to be used after other attempts fail. The formula is excellent for arbitration, and as such will be addressed in chapter 7.

For matters of church discipline one must look to other passages. Church discipline is more correctly patterned after 1 Corinthians 5. In the Corinthian case the wrong was not between two brothers. It was a public sin of immorality known throughout the community. As such it was a matter for the corporate body.

The Corinthian believers were never told to follow the procedure outlined in Matthew. The man to be censured was not to be given an opportunity for private repentance for a public act of immorality. The action of the body was not the last step to be used when all else failed. It was the first step. The church was commanded to take immediate corporate action to exclude the man from the fellowship.

By following *the formula in Matthew* one must always give

opportunity for private confession of repentance. Once it
is made, the requirements of the passage have been met.
There is no further need to bring the matter before the
body even if it is a matter of public immorality. To inter-
change admonitions without regard to specific facts surrounding those admonitions is to generate confusion.
Careful analysis of the Scripture is always necessary if it is
to be applied correctly.

We believe we may safely assume that only one action
should stop *the disciplinary process outlined in 1 Corinthians
5*—a public acknowledgement of repentance by the one to
be censured. Once that is made, certainly the exclusion
process would be interrupted. It should *not* be interrupted
on the basis of a private confession as outlined in Matthew
18.

*Can discipline be effective?* In examining those problems
faced by the church that dares to discipline, one cannot
help but acknowledge some of the problems inherent in
current Christian society. It is difficult to discipline a member when he has the freedom to walk across the street,
move his membership to another church, and go on with
his life as if nothing had happened. Churches sometimes
suffer a great deal because they receive into membership
individuals who are seeking to escape the discipline of another church.

Years ago in one of our pastorates a new couple began
appearing in the services with a remarkable degree of reg-
ularity. It was commonly known that they were members
of the church across town. The grapevine had it that both
husband and wife were under the discipline of their
church.

Eventually they made known their desire to unite with
our church, and the pastor member of this writing team
went to call. He questioned them on their reasons for leav-
ing their church. They admitted that they were currently
being disciplined. Although it was not an accusation of
serious misconduct, it was clear that the church had suf-

ficient reason to take the action. A course of action was suggested to them. "Go back and make things right with your church, and then we will be happy to consider your membership."

The couple not only took his advice, but they were also restored to fellowship within their own church. That is the ultimate goal of church discipline.

Unfortunately in too many cases no attempt is made to make things right. Consequently the disciplined members never experience restoration. Frequently they blame the pastor or the church for their predicament. Spiritual regression is the predictable result.

Jessica was one such person. Married and the mother of two small children, she became involved with the husband of her best friend. She rationalized her adultery by saying, "I prayed that we would get together, and the Lord answered my prayer."

Her pastor, upon hearing this blatant explanation, countered with "God didn't answer your prayer. You did!" Jessica showed no remorse. Rather than face discipline of the congregation, she simply asked that her name be dropped from the roll, and she never came back.

About a year later a new neighbor invited Jessica to attend church with her. It happened to be Jessica's former church. Jessica commented, "No, I'm not interested. I used to belong to that church, but the pastor and I had a personality conflict."

It is easy to rationalize, "Why bother? Discipline won't do any good anyway." Whether or not the discipline accomplishes its purpose is not the issue. The issue is responsibility. When the church carries out its responsibility, that is all that is required. How the individual responds is his responsibility.

*Lack of unity hinders discipline.* It takes unity to carry out discipline. When disunity is present the process becomes unbelievably complicated. Basically, of course, this is because wherever disunity is present, the body itself has a problem. It is also true that when disunity is a problem, people refuse to agree on any issue no matter what the facts may be.

The Corinthian church was troubled by disunity. Their pride of identity led them to criticize their spiritual leaders and to divide into little cliques within the church. It is not difficult to understand why Paul spent one fourth of his letter admonishing them to clear up their disunity before he commanded them to judge sin within the body.

*A call to discipline.* Rising immorality within the evangelical community forces the church to face the issue of discipline. Theoretically many evangelicals believe in its necessity. That is not to say that discipline is practiced to the extent it should be within the ranks of evangelical Christianity. Acknowledging responsibility is one thing. Carrying it out is another.

A sharp focus is needed to accomplish the decisive and definitive action called for. The purpose of discipline must be understood clearly by all. It is for the good of the community, the good of the church, and for the good of the disciplined individual.

As the church assumes the responsibility of exclusion, it initiates action intended to bring correction, repentance, forgiveness, and restoration.

It is not the responsibility of the church to control the end result. Instead the responsibility is to mourn over the sin that has invaded the body, exclude the sinner, and leave the results with God.

*Case history C.* A lesson could be drawn from a church in the jungles of Mexico. At this writing, this body of believers has had the Word of God in their own language only about six years. All first-generation Christians, the indigenous church has made astounding progress in spite of the hostile environment.

At one point the body faced the need to discipline one of the elders for a problem of immorality. Whether or not the church had a formal membership we do not know. But the congregation excluded him from their fellowship in a way that was clearly understood by all.

The man was required to attend all services (they determined that he needed that), but he was forced to sit on the back row (not a favored seat in the jungle church). He was forbidden to join in the singing (the worst possible punishment), and he was not allowed to partake of Communion.

In the truest sense, in that culture, he was excluded from fellowship. Not surprisingly, the man repented, discontinued his illicit relationship, and was restored to fellowship.

Church structure varies from century to century and from culture to culture. But exclusion is a word we all understand. It can be practiced in such a way that it is understood by all.

All it takes is a church that dares to discipline.

# 5

## The Commands to Refrain from Judging

To condemn or censure another human being is the action most people think of when they say, "We're never supposed to judge, are we?" Nevertheless, as has been demonstrated in the previous chapters, the corporate Body of Christ is charged with the responsibility to censure on certain occasions. About this there can be no mistake.

Just so, there can be no mistake about other passages that warn the believer against censuring or condemning. Matthew 7:1 is the classic example: "Judge not that ye be not judged." James 4:12 asks the question, "Who art thou that judgeth another?"

How does one relate these passages to 1 Corinthians 5? How is it that one passage demands censure and others warn against it? What can we learn about judging by comparing these passages?

The most obvious point of comparison is that 1 Corinthians 5 is directed to the corporate body, and the other passages are directed to individual believers. In James the believer is warned against defaming another man's character. In Matthew he is warned against hypocritical judging.

*Do not judge in a defamatory manner* (James 4:11-12). The defamatory judging addressed by James grew out of a climate of envy and strife. Apparently it had no purpose. It was carried out through aimless (and endless?) talking. The sole motivation was to censure fellow believers by passing along negative evaluations.

The focal passage is set against a background of admonitions concerning the tongue. James sees the tongue as a tool of Satan, something uncontrollable. He characterizes it as something that praises God on the one hand and curses man on the other. "This should not be!" he declares.

Through James's eyes we see the act of condemning coupled with slander. "Speak not evil one of another, brethren. He that speaketh evil of his brother and judgeth his brother. . ."

The word translated "speak evil" is *katalaleo*, which means to speak evil against, to say bad things, to slander. Another word sometimes translated "slander" is *diabolus*, from which is derived our English word "devil."

This word is used in Titus 2:3 ("false accuser") and in 1 Timothy 3:11 ("slanderer"). The word actually refers to a person who is given to finding fault with the conduct of others by spreading innuendos and criticisms in the church.

Although Christians tend to take this sin of slander lightly (as if God graded on the curve), Scripture consistently teaches that it is a very serious offense.

Consider for example that the control of the tongue was one of two specific prerequisites for the older woman in order that she might be a teacher of the younger (Titus 2:3). All women are expected to attain to the entire standard outlined in Titus 2:3-5, but the teacher is characterized as having already attained a certain control over her tongue. She was not to be a false accuser.

Slander and defamatory judging go hand in hand, according to James. This is cruel gossip, the lowest possible use of the tongue. It was the cause of dissension in the first century. It is the cause of dissension today.

Many times we have had cause to contemplate the histories of two congregations about which we have intimate knowledge. One church has had to deal with a number of moral problems over the years. Yet it has maintained a strong unity within the body and a strong testimony within the community. The other church, its history unspotted by moral problems, is characterized by division. On more than one occasion it has been torn apart as its members indulged in malicious slander. Its testimony in the community is nil.

Defamatory judgment is a pernicious practice. Fortunate indeed is the church that is populated by believers who refuse to engage in this pastime.

*Do not judge hypocritically* (Matthew 7:1-5). By examining the context of the Matthew statement, some important facts may be isolated. These facts indicate that the warning is against hypocritical judgment perpetrated by one believer against another. Specifically the passage teaches:

● The act of condemning or censuring imposes a standard upon the censured individual.
● The one who imposes a standard will be expected to live by that same standard.
● When one engages in hypocritical judging, the natural outcome is that he will in turn be judged by his fellowmen.

Judging by a double standard (one for self and one for others) not only incurs judgment by one's peers, but it also raises certain questions.

Why should you be concerned about what is going on in your brother's life and not be concerned about what is going on in your own life?

How can you straighten out your brother's life until you have first straightened out your own?

Many sincere believers look at Matthew 7:1 as an isolated passage and assume that it dictates a "live and let live" policy. But when taken in context, one may easily see that the more accurate interpretation is "Take care of your own life in order that you may be in a position to help others."

Verse 4 asks how you can tell your brother you will pull the speck out of his eye when there is a board in your own. Verse 5 gives instructions for the disposition of both board and speck—get rid of the board in your own eye so you can see to take the speck out of your brother's.

Certainly it should never be assumed that either the board or the speck should become permanent fixtures. The ideal resolution is for both to be removed.

This passage speaks as strongly of the perpetrator as of the act. It is not saying that every act of correction is wrong. It is saying that not everyone is qualified to correct another believer.

This principle is reiterated in Galatians 6:1-2. Here the believer who is spiritual is urged to help other believers clean up their lives. The spiritually mature are charged with the responsibility of restoring fallen believers.

The implication is that there must be a gentle confrontation. The mature believer is warned that he should proceed out of a spirit of humility, keeping in mind his own potential to be tempted. This insures against hypocritical judgment.

Thus, the Scriptures provide their own best commentary. By comparing a number of passages we find that the harshest censure is to be meted out only by the corporate church body. Even then the final judging is in God's hand. The responsibility of the church is to exclude. The responsibility of the individual is to carry out the exclusion dictated by the church.

We also find that it is the responsibility of mature believers to seek to restore fallen believers. That restoration can neither precede nor circumvent church action in cases demanding discipline by the corporate body.

Finally we are forced to conclude that the Scriptures do not give a directive against all judging. Instead they warn against hypocritical judging, double standards, and senseless slander.

The Christian who cares enough to confront must also be a Christian who carefully keeps his own life in order.

# DIVISION II:

# JUDGING THAT INVOLVES ARBITRATION

In 1 Corinthians 6 the word *krino* is used in connection with another word, *kriterion*. This word, a noun, denotes a court of justice or a tribunal.

First Corinthians 6:1-8 deals with the responsibility of the church to judge disputes among believers.

Arbitration as pictured in this passage may be defined as the settling of a dispute through the use of a third party or parties. Three Greek words are used in the passage. The use of the word *diakrino* (verse 5) leads us to believe that those called upon to arbitrate should possess acute skills in making judgments.

# 6

## I Won't Go to Court—He's My Brother!

"I don't believe in churches going to court to settle disputes," said the man sitting across the room. The statement was not unusual since many Christians have strong convictions along this line; however the events leading to this counseling session give the incident special significance.

The counselee, Jim Alexander, was not a member of our church. He was a layman from a church a few miles distant. Everyone in the general vicinity had watched his church deteriorate through an internal struggle over doctrinal differences. Jim, along with his sister and brother-in-law, was the recognized leader of the dissension group.

Within two years the church had departed from its stated doctrinal position. Many families left, and Alexander's group emerged as the majority. Nothing remained of the church as it had been conceived except the name and three families who stood by the original doctrinal position. Even the pastor had joined Alexander's group. It had been a very heated and very public dispute.

A climax came when several of Alexander's followers proposed a change of name for the church and an official declaration of a change of doctrine. The three remaining families of the original group declared, "We'll take you to court." Legal proceedings were initiated.

A strange thing happened. Alexander decided it was wrong to go to court. As he sat in the office of our church he made clear that he would not go along with a court battle because of the scriptural admonition in 1 Corinthians 6.

He also made clear that he did not regret the fact that he had been party to the infiltration of the church with contrary doctrine. He felt no guilt over the chaos within the church over the previous two years. He only felt pangs of conscience over going to court. "After all, First Corinthians six says that Christians aren't supposed to go to court, doesn't it?"

The question is, does a Christian fulfill the admonition in 1 Corinthians 6 by refusing to go to court against a fellow believer?

Not really.

In taking 1 Corinthians 6:7 by itself, the reader mistakenly assumes the emphasis to be that believers should not go to law against one another. But a look at the whole shows the major emphasis to be that the church should be practicing the art of arbitration.

Three facts are indicated in the passage. (1) A third party, or parties, should be enlisted to act as judge, tribunal, or court. (2) This party, or parties, must possess the ability to make acute judgment. This is indicated by the use of the Greek *diakrino* in verse 5. (3) The function of the party, or parties, is to make a judgment by which the disputing parties will abide.

When disputes between believers are handled correctly, it is not necessary to take the question before unbelievers (i.e., a court of law).

Paul rebuked the Corinthians for their negligence in

settling personal disputes. He reminded them that believers will one day judge the world, assuming all legal aspects of Christ's Kingdom. It would seem then that Christians should be able to judge matters within their own peer group.

In addition, Paul pointed to the fact that believers will be called upon to judge angels. Certainly they should be able to judge things pertaining to this life. Why enlist the aid of unregenerate people?

The passage conjures up a scenario. Imagine the believers of the First Church of Corinth saying, "One day we are going to be responsible for judging the world. In fact we are even going to judge angels. But right now we can't settle this little matter. We will ask these unregenerate Corinthian people to decide who is right or wrong here."

To resort to such a practice is an admission that there is no one within the church who is wise enough to judge disputes among the believers. What a shame!

Such an admission of failure is indicative of a serious problem within the body. In fact it would be far better to take the wrong than to go to court.

However, the suggestion that the believer take wrong rather than go to court against another believer should not be interpreted as a suggested solution to the problem. The real solution is arbitration. The apostle is not saying, "Take wrong in order to resolve your problem." He is saying, "Practice the art of arbitration to resolve your disputes. Going to court is not an option for believers."

The passage opens with the reminder that the saints will judge legal matters in the Kingdom; it closes with the reminder that the unregenerate will not inherit the Kingdom. In between, the apostle reminds the believers how far they have come. Through the saving grace of God they had come from the depths of sin to new life in Christ. As believers they share nothing with the unbelievers—not even a common destiny. Why, then, should they depend upon unbelievers for wisdom to solve their disputes?

Certainly this passage declares that a believer should not go to law against another believer. But more than that it communicates that if Christians would practice arbitrating disputes between themselves it would never come to the point of a legal battle. To refuse to go to court is to obey but half of the directive. The emphasis is on the positive act of arbitration rather than on the negative act of not going to court.

The importance of this principle can be seen as one observes relationships within a local church. Strained personal relationships quickly affect the body as a whole.

We once observed a church in which two members had a business disagreement of long standing. Neither felt it right to go to court with their dispute. But no attempt was made to arbitrate the disagreement. Over the years bitterness and resentment grew between the two. Of course their personal problem took its toll on the unity of the church.

It is never enough to say, "I won't go to court—he's my brother." The action called for is a resolving of the difference by asking some wise person (or persons) in the church to arbitrate.

Matthew 18:15 gives a workable principle for arbitration. That will be considered in the following chapter.

# 7

## A Biblical Plan for Arbitration
### (Matthew 18:15-17)

The purpose of biblical arbitration is neither to establish guilt nor to exact punishment. It is to effect reconciliation between the offended and the offender.

In their book *Tell It to the Church,* Lynn Buzzard and Laurence Eck have this to say about reconciliation: "The church surely has the calling, the church has the concepts, the church has the gifts, and the church has the Lord. All that remains is for the church to have the will to hear the call of Scripture for the reconciled to be agents of reconciliation."[1]

*The scriptural formula for arbitration.* In the area of reconciliation (as in many other areas) the responsibility of the church begins with the responsibility of the individuals who make up the church. The formula for scriptural arbitration calls for up to three steps, and it all begins with one person. Matthew 18:15-17 states the formula.

1. Lynn Buzzard and Laurence Eck, *Tell It to the Church* (Elgin, Ill.: David C. Cook, 1982), p. 16. Used by permission. Copyright 1982 Lynn Buzzard. David C. Cook Publishing Co., Elgin, IL 60120.

Moreover if thy brother shall trespass against thee, go
and tell him his fault between thee and him alone: if
he shall hear thee, thou hast gained thy brother. But if
he will not hear thee, then take with thee one or two
more, that in the mouth of two or three witnesses every
word may be established. And if he shall neglect to hear
them, tell it unto the church: but if he neglect to hear
the church, let him be unto thee as a heathen man and
a publican.

*Step one.* It is the responsibility of the offended party to
(1) seek out the offender, (2) tell him what he has done,
(3) tell it to him in private, and (4) try to effect a reconciliation without involving others.

How often the very opposite is true! If the offended seeks
out the offender at all, it is only after the offense has been
made known to the entire church and half the town.

*Step two.* If the offender does not listen when privately
confronted, then the offended is to return with one or more
witnesses. It should be understood that these witnesses are
mature believers who can act objectively. Their function is
twofold—to witness the sincere attempt at reconciliation
and to assist in arbitration.

*Step three.* The final step, if all else fails, is to tell it to the
church. The offended and witness(es) report the incident
and previous attempts at reconciliation. Again, the purpose
is to effect a reconciliation between the two parties. This
step also absolves the offended of further responsibility
should the final attempt fail. He can rest assured he has
exhausted his resources and has acted responsibly, albeit
without results.

There is value in the formula for all concerned. When
followed, the formula prevents widespread knowledge of
that which should be a private matter. It allows the offender
to make things right without having to defend himself to
half the town.

The formula has the potential for strengthening the relationship between two individuals. The phrase "thou has gained a brother" is a significant comment on relationships. Many individuals have found a deepened relationship after they took the initiative to open communication through a private, often painful, confrontation.

The formula can be interrupted at any step. When a reconciliation is accomplished there is no further need to expose the problem. It involves others only after a personal, private attempt fails. It involves the church body only as a final step.

The formula is not offered with a guarantee. But if followed correctly, the offended has peace of mind in his assurance that he has done his best.

*Avoiding error in application.* In applying Matthew 18:15-17 as a formula for arbitration, several facts should be noted. (1) The offense was between two individual believers. One brother had trespassed against (sinned against, offended) another brother. It was not a sin against the church body. It probably was not a public matter. (2) The action was to be initiated to resolve a difference. It was not to establish guilt or to exact punishment. (3) The action was to be initiated by the offended.

Error in application must be avoided. The formula is not to be seen as a pattern for church discipline in cases calling for action by the body. Certainly this formula must never be applied to circumvent action such as that called for in 1 Corinthians 5.

In addition, the third step, "tell it to the church," must be understood as a valid step for arbitration between two believers. This step is not contingent upon the seriousness of the offense. It is contingent upon the seriousness of the breach. It should never be reserved exclusively for cases in which the church is widely affected. The offense to the church is not the question. Offense between two believers is the issue. The church is simply the vehicle through which the reconciliation attempt is being made.

*Christian Conciliation Service.* In the twentieth century,

disputes between believers often involve more than one local church body. Christians who work together and fellowship together do not necessarily worship in the same church. How can the Matthew formula be applied if step one fails to produce the desired results? From which church will the third party (or parties) be chosen? The Christian Conciliation Service affords a possible solution.

This concept, which is gaining popularity, is designed to cross denominational lines. The plan calls for a conciliation committee made up of Christian attorneys from several churches. An outgrowth of the Christian Legal Society, the CCS has established a number of chapters throughout the United States.

*Attitude and reconciliation.* Whether the reconciliation attempt is handled within the local church or through a Christian Conciliation Service, the attitude of the respective parties is crucial to success. Many conciliation groups begin their reconciliation attempt by counseling the involved parties with regard to attitude.

It is quite obvious from the Matthew passage that unless the offender responds with the right attitude, the attempt will fail. The attitude of the offended is equally important.

It is important to remember that chronologically, Matthew 18 follows the Sermon on the Mount. Christ has already stipulated that He came to fulfill the law. Throughout the gospels and the epistles we are taught that love is the fulfilling of the law. Certainly when it comes to offenses, love must be the basis for responsible action.

*Love's responsibility toward offenses.* Matthew 18:15-17 is part of a greater passage in which our Lord deals with two sides of the subject of offense. Christ wanted His followers to maintain an attitude of loving responsibility in matters of offense. He left a double challenge to believers. (1) Don't be an offense to fellow believers. (2) Do make every attempt to restore a loving relationship with a believer who has offended you.

The greater passage, Matthew 18:1-17, presents an interesting contrast to Deuteronomy 19. Many commentaries take note that Matthew 18:16 is a quotation from Deuteronomy 19:15. But they only note the similarity—"in the mouth of two or three witnesses every word may be established." Equally important is the difference in the two passages.

In Deuteronomy the role of the witness was to establish the guilt of the offender. In Matthew the witness was to verify an attempt at reconciliation with one's offender. Deuteronomy deals with rights under the law. Matthew deals with responsibility under love.

In Christ's challenge "Don't be an offense!" He also alluded to Deuteronomy 19. Under the law the offender was punished, after guilt was established, according to the crime. The law demanded life for life, eye for eye, tooth for tooth, hand for hand, foot for foot (Deuteronomy 19:21).

Under love, Christ challenged His followers to impose judgment upon themselves rather than be an offense. In metaphorical language He charged them to be ruthless in self judgment—cut off your hand, cut off your foot, pluck out your eye rather than play the role of an offender.

*Arbitration essential to worship.* Arbitration is essential to the spiritual and emotional health of Christians. This is true for the offended and the offender alike. In the long run it is also true for the church. Optimum health of the body is contingent upon the health of its member parts.

Matthew 5:23-24 implies that a reconciliation with one's brother is essential to acceptable worship. Certainly we may assume that any disobedience hinders personal worship. This includes unresolved differences if the difference has been ignored and no attempt at reconciliation has been made.

Many churches see no necessity to encourage settlement of personal disputes. The body proceeds with "business as usual" while trying to ignore obvious problems among members. Buzzard and Eck observe that churches usually select the first option and run from conflict. They seek, sometimes at all costs, to avoid conflicts. They do not want to own them at all. They wish they would go away. They have enough troubles of their own without becoming involved in other people's. [2]

It is well to remember that the mark of a believer is love for another believer. Such love cannot thrive where Christians ignore the scriptural command concerning reconciliation.

*Suggested Resources*
Lynn R. Buzzard and Laurence Eck, *Tell It to the Church* (Elgin, Ill.: David C. Cook, 1982). A rather complete handbook. Discusses need for Christian conciliation, provides samples for arbitration agreements and a Bible study for preparing participants.

Christian Legal Society
P.O. Box 2069
Oak Park, Illinois 60303
(312) 848-7735
Contact for information on Christian Conciliation Service including location of chapters in U.S.

2. Ibid., p. 25.

# DIVISION III

# MAKING JUDGMENTS: CRITICAL EVALUATION

Believers are called upon daily to make judgments pertaining to personal life-style and to relationships with others. Such judgments must be made by weighing one fact against another and coming to a decision.

The ability to make judgments is a skill to be pursued. Paul encouraged the development of this skill among early Christians. Often he answered their questions by stating facts and principles by which the believers could determine their own answers.

This process of making judgments may be called critical evaluation. For the most part, whenever critical evaluation is involved, we see the Greek word *anakrino*. This word is often used of a preliminary hearing, when facts are weighed.

The issues with which the early Christians struggled differ from those issues demanding critical evaluation in the current era, but the principles by which Paul instructed believers to weigh the facts are just as applicable today.

For the purpose of this book we have chosen to isolate three major areas in which Christians are called upon to make critical evaluations.

● How do I know if I am to leave all and follow Jesus?

● How should I relate to people with differing convictions about life-style?

● Can something that is right for other believers ever be wrong for me?

Principles for making these judgments are drawn from three passages of Scripture—1 Corinthians 7, Romans 14, and 1 Corinthians 8-10.

# 8

## Can Anything Be More Important Than Serving the Lord?
### (1 Corinthians 7)

There is, perhaps, nothing more unsettling than a brand new Christian who has suddenly determined to leave all and follow Jesus. Fiercely grasping this single concept, the new believer determines to shed all earthly responsibilities in order to pursue a heavenly goal. Even as I admire such zeal, I cringe at the total lack of judgment.

I cringe even more at the lack of judgment evidenced by admiring older Christians caught up by the excitement of a zealous young Christian.

We once watched a group of older Christians become completely irrational in the wake of a new believer's unrestrained zeal. Although they were quite intelligent under normal circumstances, their reasoning powers were clouded by their unequivocal admiration for Jerry, a new Christian with one consuming goal—to serve the Lord completely.

One night Jerry quietly disappeared. Even though his wedding was just weeks away he left no plausible explanation for his fiancee, only a Scripture verse taped to the steering wheel of his abandoned car. It read, ". . .they forsook their nets and followed him."

Within hours the admiring older friends had convinced themselves that Jerry surely must have been raptured. Like Enoch, this young man was truly walking with the Lord. How else could one explain such a sudden disappearance? This bizarre case ended on a happy note when Jerry returned, and the wedding took place on schedule. In time, Jerry acquired the skill of making sound judgments, and our older friends have not made any wild conjectures about one-on-one raptures since that incident.

Over the years we have seen other less sensational cases in which Christians have struggled with the question "How can I serve the Lord more completely?"

"I'm sure God is calling me to be a missionary, but my husband is not a Christian. How can I obey the Lord?"

"I want to sell my business and go to Bible college, but my wife is an unbeliever. Don't I have an obligation to pursue my vision?"

Recently we saw this statement in print: "I have divorced my wife because the Lord has called me to a life of celibacy."

For Christians of this mindset, 1 Corinthians 7 provides abiding principles by which one may make correct judgments. The first-century recipients of this letter also struggled with questions regarding serving the Lord. Some determined that one should shed all trappings of this world in order to pursue a divine calling. Apparently in addressing the question "What could be more important than serving the Lord?" they concluded that the ideal life-style was one of celibacy.

Reaching that ideal presented something of a problem, since many believers were already married at the time of their conversion. Thus they struggled with questions about marriage, divorce, and divine service.

"Wouldn't it be better not to be married?"

"Couldn't I serve the Lord more effectively as a single?"

"Should a believer leave an unbelieving spouse?"

"Should a believer seek to be released from an engagement?" (This was a binding commitment in New Testament times.)

*First things first.* Like their modern-day counterparts, the Corinthians had many concerns about marriage but few compunctions about adulterous relations. By their own admission, they were unable to judge whether, in a sensual society, they should be married. Before answering their specific questions, Paul first concerned himself with teaching them a new respect for the human body. Until the believers clearly understood the implications of sexual sin they would be unable to make proper judgments about the questions they faced.

As a city of vice and debauchery, Corinth had no rival in Roman time. Her citizens worshiped numbers of gods and goddesses. But their greatest devotion was reserved for Aphrodite, the goddess of love. More than 1,000 prostitutes served in her temple.

To believers emerging from this background, Paul was compelled to communicate that the body is not for fornication. This appears in 1 Corinthians 6:9-20, which serves as a bridge between two major subjects. In this passage Paul contrasts believers with unbelievers. Sexual sin is the most frequently named characteristic of unbelievers. Some of the Corinthian believers had once been so characterized. But through a conversion experience they had been made clean, whole, and different. Clearly, God expected such a change to take place in all believers.

According to 6:18, sexual sin is set apart from all other sins. That is not to say that it cannot be forgiven or that it carries an irremovable stigma. (First John 1:9 applies to all sin.) However, the fact that Paul chose to separate it from other sin cannot be missed. It is a fact that demands grave consideration.

"Every sin man commits is without the body, but fornication is committed against one's own body," Paul declared. Then, calling upon their powers of reasoning, he posed four questions to make his point.

- "Don't you know your bodies are members (body parts) of Christ?"
- "Would you willingly join Christ's members to that of a harlot?" (God forbid!)
- "Don't you know when one is joined to a harlot he is one with her because in the sexual union two become one?"
- "Don't you know that your body is the dwelling place of the Holy Spirit?"

In addition to these questions, Paul made a number of statements regarding the body. In summation, there are at least three reasons sexual sin is different from other sin.

First, it is different because of the unique relationship of the believer's body to Christ. Second, it is different because of the unique relationship of two people joined by the sexual act. Third, it is different because of the unique relationship of the believer's body to the Holy Spirit.

As Paul concludes his reasoning he moves immediately into his next subject. Notice how it flows.

"You are not your own because you are bought with a price; therefore glorify God in your body and in your spirit. Now concerning the things about which you wrote to me. It is good for a man not to touch a woman, nevertheless to avoid fornication. . ."

Having laid the groundwork, Paul now moves on to show how principles concerning sexual purity relate to questions about serving the Lord.

*Obedience a higher priority than service.* God has specifically revealed His standards concerning sexual relationships. Paul shows how obedience to this standard takes priority over service. His very practical admonitions in 1 Corinthians 7 are addressed to Christian couples, to singles, to the widowed, and to the Christian who is married to an unsaved spouse.

To the couples Paul declares that the wife has an obligation to her husband. Likewise the husband has an obligation to his wife. Speaking of sexual obligations to one another, he stresses the need to be aware of spousal needs. Meeting those needs avoids fornication.

Abstaining from sexual relations to allow time for fasting and prayer may sound very pious, but Paul cautions that such abstinence should be by mutual consent. Spousal needs must be considered and a time limit set in order to avoid unnecessary temptation.

In addressing the questions posed by the Corinthians, Paul's primary emphasis is that sexual purity is a higher priority than divine service. Lest that be misinterpreted, let it be noted that there is a distinction between serving God and obeying God. Many a Christian, past and present, has conscientiously offered his service to God while steadfastly withholding his obedience.

*Celibacy is not for everyone.* The apostle readily acknowledges that single people can serve the Lord with more freedom. They do not have the spousal and familial obligations of married believers. But the fact that celibate life is less encumbered should never lead a believer to make unwise decisions. For example, a Christian should not sever a marriage relationship in order to pursue a divine calling. Nor should a Christian seek to remain single if he does not possess the gift of celibacy.

As for those cases in which one partner has become a Christian and the other remains an unbeliever, Paul relays God's command. "Don't leave your mate." Although this union may indeed limit the service of the Christian spouse, the believer is not to seek to dissolve it.

The apostle acknowledges there may be cases in which an unbelieving spouse chooses to leave; however the implication is that the action should never be precipitated by the Christian's neglect of spousal needs.

For the already married, the issue of celibacy is settled. Those believers have no such option. There is no need to struggle with a decision.

The single or the widowed may opt for celibacy. But

believers in this category must carefully consider the question "Can I control my sexual desires?"

Engaged couples were considered separately. They had more options than the married, but fewer than the widowed or uncommitted single. There was no revealed directive from God on how a betrothed should handle the question. But Paul gave his critical evaluation.

The passage 7:34-38 seems to indicate that in some cases an individual could be released from the engagement. Others would not have that option. Decisions would have to be made on the basis of facts involved. Paul encouraged those in this category to make a judgment (verse 37, "decreed in his own heart").

Throughout the passage, this apostle communicates that it is easier to serve the Lord with fewer responsibilities. But God is more interested in obedience than in service. Obedience demands sexual purity.

Can you control your sexual desires? If not, do not seek a life of celibacy. Were you already married when you became a Christian? Then the celibate life is not for you. In fact your basic obligation is to guard against fornication by meeting the sexual needs of your spouse.

*Circumstances, options, and service.* When one experiences conversion, one's circumstances may be different from that of fellow believers. Those circumstances may eliminate certain options such as the mission field, Bible college, "full-time service," and so on. But circumstances will never eliminate all service. Each believer can serve the Lord in some way wherever God finds him.

The key to the passage may be found in 7:17. "Wherever the Lord found you, serve Him there." In modern vernacular it translates "Bloom where you are planted."

To illustrate, the apostle points to the fact that some are born Jewish. Some are born Gentiles. Some are born slaves. Certainly they did not all have the same options. But all could serve the Lord after rebirth.

The passage should do away forever with the "if only" mindset.

"If only I had not married before I became a Christian."

"If only I could be a missionary in Africa!"

"If only I had been born into a Christian home."

"If only I were someone else, or some place else, then I could serve the Lord with all of my energies."

Paul refutes this concept by showing that personal circumstances have little to do with dedicated service.

The record reveals, then, that the Corinthian Christians had a problem relating their Christianity to daily living. Apparently neither personal wisdom nor preferred leaders could solve that problem. For although they boasted of wisdom and of favorite leaders who were much more eloquent than Paul, when it came to making judgments about their life-style, they turned to the apostle. He was called upon to arbitrate, to answer questions, and to advise.

Paul's chief desire was that the believers would develop within themselves the ability to make intelligent spiritual judgments. He was not content to answer their specific questions. Instead he taught them how to balance scriptural principles with other scriptural principles in order to make decisions about everyday living.

Many people look at 1 Corinthians 7 as the last word on marriage and divorce. Contextually this seems doubtful. We see it instead as the last word on the relationship between sexual purity and divine service.

With conjugal relationships between unmarried Christians on the rise, it is time to sound a warning to believers everywhere—God is more interested in your obedience than in your service.

# 9

# What Is
# My Responsibility
# Regarding Another
# Believer's Conscience?
### (Romans 14)

Throughout church history, Christians have had to deal with issues for which there are only inconclusive answers. The Scriptures are not silent. But they halt short of directives.

In the early church it was meat and holy days. Should a believer eat meat offered to idols? Should he observe holy days? In the twentieth-century church it may be dress code, entertainment, music, or wine consumption.

Left without specific commands, believers divide themselves over these debatable issues. Convictions vary according to individual conscience.

How should one arrive at a decision when no clear command is given? Several theories persist. On the one extreme is the contention that the church should take a firm stand on everything. On the other extreme is the feeling that a Christian is completely free to do anything conscience allows.

The goal of the first theory is to eliminate debatable

issues through conformity. The church that takes a stand on everything determines for each believer what he should wear, how he should cut his hair, where he should go, and with whom he should associate. There is little need for any member to be concerned about convictions (his or others), because those things are predetermined.

Although Paul constantly urged Christians to develop a pure standard of living, he was ever anxious that they arrive at that standard without the crutch of legalism. He did not teach that forced conformity was the answer to debatable issues. Instead he gave facts and principles and called for Christians to make critical evaluations.

The goal of the second theory seems to be to eliminate absolutes and insure for every Christian the liberty to "do his own thing." Paul's writings to the Romans (14:13-14) are often erroneously used as a proof text for those believers who insist upon their freedom to do whatever conscience allows. "You're not supposed to judge," the liberated one insists. "If you think it's wrong, then it's wrong for you. I may not share the same convictions."

Misquoted, misunderstood, and misinterpreted, those two verses have become the basis for the live-and-let-live policy adopted by liberated Christians.

> Let us not therefore judge one another any more: but judge this rather, that no man put a stumblingblock or an occasion to fall in his brother's way. I know, and am persuaded by the Lord Jesus, that there is nothing unclean of itself: but to him that esteemeth any thing to be unclean, to him it is unclean.

In truth, Paul is not communicating here about taking liberty. He is communicating about giving liberty. This becomes quite clear when the passage is studied in context. A proper understanding of the greater passage will enable believers of any age to make proper judgments about debatable issues.

Essentially Paul gives two principles regarding debatable issues. (1) Do not judge those whose convictions are less stringent than yours. (2) Do not offend those whose convictions are more stringent.

*Proper application of the principle.* Proper application of these principles necessitates a warning. The Roman problem was neither doctrinal nor moral. The principles do not apply to questions specifically covered in the Scriptures. In other words there are many nondebatable items. A believer's conviction (or lack of conviction) does not determine the rightness or wrongness of matters specifically covered by God's Word. Nor are obedient Christians called upon to tolerate biblically unacceptable conduct or doctrine perpetrated by fellow believers who suffer from a lack of conviction. The twofold principle applies only to *morally neutral issues.*

With that warning fully understood, let us examine the Christian's responsibility for his fellow believer's conscience.

*Receive one another.* That was Paul's first admonition to the Romans concerning disputable matters. The church at Rome was made up of both herb eaters and meat eaters. Each group acted upon personal conviction.

Paul could have said, "Organize two congregations—one for the herb eaters and one for meat eaters." Or he could have urged the church to take a unified stand and insist that all members conform. Instead he encouraged them to receive and to respect one another.

To the meat eaters he said, "Receive the herb eaters" (14:1-2). To the herb eaters he said, "Don't judge the meat eaters" (verse 3). He cautioned them that conscience should be one's guide (verse 5) and that whether eating or abstaining, the believer should live as unto the Lord (verses 6-8).

Romans 14:1 (as well as 1 Corinthians 8:10) characterizes the weaker believer as one who has stricter taboos. This can sometimes be misunderstood or misused.

One young minister, speaking to a group of high school students challenged, "If you are offended by what I do, then you are the weaker Christian." Specifically he named a habit generally considered unacceptable by those families represented in his audience. The statement evoked strong reaction from several students whose standards were notably higher than the status quo. The ripple set off among the students soon made waves into the parental circle. "How can he say that?" asked one bewildered mother. "Where does he get that?"

Although the statement touched on a biblical truth, it failed to communicate the true intent of the Scripture. First of all, it was applied too broadly. Second, one can hardly assume that the passage was intended to give liberated Christians an opportunity to point a finger and say, "You're weak!" To the contrary, the passage is intended to encourage responsibility toward fellow believers.

*Recognizing personal responsibility.* Paul is very graphic as he discusses the effect of individual liberty upon the conscience of fellow believers. Personal liberty must never be used to run roughshod over another's conscience.

The apostle sees as evidence of true Christian strength one's sensitivity toward other believers. The test of that strength is not how strongly one holds one's convictions. Nor is it how liberated a believer may be in Christ. The test of Christian strength is how well one protects his fellow believer's conscience.

It is difficult for some Christians to grasp this concept. "I drink wine with a clear conscience," one believer remarked. "If I abstain on some occasion just because I might offend some other Christian, doesn't that make me a hypocrite?"

There is nothing hypocritical about respecting another believer's conscience.

We are not dealing with a case of pretending to be something you are not. It seems obvious from the passage that the herb eaters knew who the meat eaters were and vice versa. But the apostle challenged them not to do anything in front of another believer that would offend him or cause him to stumble. "Don't flaunt your faith in front of others who might be hurt by it" is Kenneth Taylor's rendition of Romans 14:22.

*Recognize the role of the conscience.* Fully half of the chapter may be seen to relate to the conscience. Isolating the directives in the passage shows how important it is to honor one's own conscience and to respect the convictions of a fellow believer's conscience. Note these directives.

• Receive the weak believer (and don't argue with him, verse 1).

• Do not despise (look down upon) the herb eater (verse 3).

• Do not judge the meat eater (verse 3).

• Let every man be fully pursuaded in his own mind (verse 5).

• Do not judge one another (i.e., in this matter, verse 13).

• Judge this: Are you a stumbling block to a fellow believer (verse 13)?

• Do not destroy by your liberty that believer for whom Christ died (verse 15).

• Try to keep peace and edify one another (verse 19).

• Do not partake in that which your conscience condemns (verses 20, 23).

• Do not partake in that which will cause a brother to stumble (verse 21).

• Do not flaunt your liberty (verse 22).

An important cross reference may be found in 1 Corinthians 8:6-7, 13. In this passage Paul points to the danger of using one's liberty to encourage a fellow believer to go against his conscience. His conclusion is "If eating meat offends my brother, I will eat no meat."

The strength as well as the intent of this conclusion is obscured by our limited understanding of the word *offense*.

Webster defines it as that which causes one to "feel hurt, resentful, or angry." Applying this definition does little to clarify the relationship of herb eaters and meat eaters. In fact, it allows for enslavement of meat eaters by their legalistic herb-eating brothers, who may be given to feeling hurt or angry. It also effectively relieves herb eaters of their responsibility to withhold judgment of meat eaters.

For a better understanding we must consider the original language. The Greek word used in 1 Corinthians 8:13 is *skandalizo*, signifying to put a snare or stumbling block in the way. Originally the noun, *skandalon*, was the name of the part of a trap to which bait is attached. The picture is that the very use of one's liberty baits the trap that snares the weaker Christian.

We may conclude that Paul is talking about a serious offense to the conscience of a fellow believer. This is not a simple matter of one Christian's disapproving of another Christian's life-style. It is a matter of one believer's being persuaded to go against his conscience through his observation of another believer's action.

It is essential that a believer not violate his conscience. In time, an herb-eating Christian may work through all the information and principles regarding eating meat. He may eventually come to a more liberated stand on the matter. Until that time, however, he should abstain. Until that time, no liberated meat eater should encourage (through word or action) the herb eater to violate his conscience.

"Conscience," states C.E. Luthardt, "is the last thing left to a man after he has squandered and lost all else that God has given him. It is the last tie by which God still retains a hold upon the man who has erred and strayed from Him and by which He reminds him of the home he has forsaken."[1]

Currently the issue of wine consumption is one of the

---

1. C.E. Luthardt, *Apologetic Lectures on the Moral Truths of Christianity* trans. Sophia Taylor, 4th ed. (Edinburgh: T.&T. Clark, 1872), p. 53. Quoted from Carl F. Henry, *Christian Personal Ethics* (Grand Rapids: Eerdmans, 1957), p. 520.

great disputable matters among believers. There are those who believe in total abstinence. Others have no such convictions.

Among those Christians whom I most admire is one woman who, in the past, was not a total abstainer by conviction. Then one day the Lord thrust her into a ministry. At that point she reexamined the question of wine consumption in relationship to its effect upon those to whom she ministered. She came to the conclusion that she should set aside her liberty in this area rather than risk being a stumbling block to one of those to whom she ministers.

In our opinion, the greatest question Christians must face regarding wine is not whether it is right or wrong in itself. The greatest question is "What will the effect of my action be upon other believers?"

A crucial problem with the wine question is one of sensitivity toward Christians whose past includes alcoholism. Certainly most of us know at least one Christian who daily looks into the mirror and admits "I am an alcoholic. I cannot drink." Coping with the problem means having no liquor in the house and staying away from office parties. Must such Christians also be tempted from the least expected source—their circle of Christian friends? In accepting an invitation to dinner will they place themselves in a high risk area of temptation because the fare includes wine?

The consumption of wine will continue to be relegated to the disputable issues category. But responsibility toward other believers is not disputable. It is always a tragedy to place a stumbling block in the way of another believer, be it through wine or any disputable matter.

*Love overrules liberty.* Contextually, Romans 14 examines the effects of love and points to Christ as the supreme example of one who pleased not Himself. Chapter 13 shows that love is the fulfillment of the law. The one who truly loves his neighbor will not do anything to harm that neighbor (verses 9-10).

Following chapter 14, in which meat eaters and herb eaters are admonished to receive and respect one another, Paul commands, "Let everyone of you please his neighbor for his edification" (15:2). He points to Christ's example, prays that the God of patience and consolation will help them become of one mind, and concludes once again with the admonition "Receive one another, as Christ has received us."

Just as love fulfills the law, so love must control liberty. Showing love is more important than seizing liberty.

For the twentieth-century church, eating meat that has been offered to idols is not a burning issue. But every church era has had its unique set of disputable matters.

What is it in your circle of Christian friends? On which side of the issue do you stand? Would you classify yourself as a meat eater or an herb eater? How do you handle differences?

When it comes to making judgments about disputable matters, every believer should consider these three facts.

- Each believer has the liberty to make his own choice.
- A believer should never act against his own conscience.
- Improper exercise of liberty has the potential of seriously damaging the conscience of another believer.

The most important judgment you will make regarding a disputable matter is not, "Is it right or wrong?" It is, "Will this be a problem to another believer?"

Disputable matters are rarely settled. Paul never concluded that it was right or wrong to eat meat. Instead he left with the believers this incontestable principle—it is wrong to destroy a person for whom Christ died.

# 10

## Can Something Right Ever Be Wrong for Me?
### (1 Corinthians 8-10)

Although the issues have changed, twentieth-century believers still struggle with questions surrounding that which is permissible and that which is good. Some are blatant with their liberty—"I will go anywhere my friends are, pot parties, beer parlors, and so on, and show by my presence that I'm approachable and have something they do not have." On the other extreme are those who believe that Christians should avoid all unnecessary contact with the world.

"If it's in style, don't wear it. If it's fun, don't do it. If unsaved people will be there, don't go." With vague mutterings about a "poor testimony," they express their adamant opinions of unacceptable activities.

A Christian who consistently and purposely avoids any contact with unbelievers will make little impact upon the world in which he lives.

On the other hand, twentieth-century liberated meat eaters often enter into situations that are easily misinterpreted, an offense to other believers, and a source of needless temptation.

Often these twentieth-century meat eaters and herb eaters have less respect for each other than their first-century counterparts. Each group needs to find the balance between unlimited liberty and restrictive legalism. Finding such a balance requires good judgment.

First Corinthians 8-10 provides additional principles whereby a believer may distinguish between that which is permissible and that which is good.

Like the Romans, the Corinthians had questions regarding meat offered to idols. Paul's lengthy answer to them emphasizes the need for believers to develop good judgment. It also confronts believers of every age with the fact that something that is right can sometimes be wrong for the individual.

As in his letter to the Romans, Paul declared that one's liberty must never be exercised to the detriment of another believer. In addition he gave the Corinthians two other principles by which to judge when right becomes wrong.

• A permissible activity is wrong if it places you in a high risk area for temptation (10:12-14).

• A permissible activity is wrong if it causes you to compromise (10:15-21).

These principles become clear as one examines the three specific warnings the apostle gave to the Corinthian meat eaters.

*Warning #1. Knowledge is liberating, but it can lead to pride.* That knowledge is liberating, there can be no doubt. The informed believer enjoys more liberty than the uniformed (1 Corinthians 8:1-8). For the Corinthians that liberty came through knowledge of some basic facts:

• An idol is nothing.
• There is only one God.

● Eating meat, or abstaining from eating, does not affect one's relationship with God.

By contrast, Paul pointed out that those without such knowledge were conscience-stricken over eating meat offered to idols (verse 7). It was important for them to abstain.

The apostle established that there is nothing wrong with eating meat, but he warned that knowledge leads to pride and that love must take precedence over liberating knowledge (verse 1). When liberty is exercised with total disregard for those who have not liberating knowledge, then liberty quickly turns to license.

At great length Paul demonstrated that he had willingly put aside his rights for the sake of others (chapter 9) and encouraged the Corinthians to follow his example.

As with the Romans, Paul's concern for the Corinthian believers was that their liberty would not become a stumbling block to weaker believers. Unlike the Roman situation, the weight of the Corinthian problem centered on actual attendance of believers at heathen religious feasts. Not only was this potentially offensive to other believers, but there was also inherent danger involved for the Christian who frequented such feasts.

*Warning #2. Liberty gives an illusion of strength.* His second warning regarding liberty had to do with the liberated believer's potential to fall into temptation. Through an illustration from Israel's past, Paul showed that in spite of spiritual blessings, in spite of knowledge, there is always a danger of temptation (10:1-11).

He then pointed out the potential for temptation that existed at heathen feasts. He warned the believers against the illusion of strength that is sometimes found in liberty. Just when a believer is confident that he is strong, that is when he will fall.

The reality of temptation must be faced. High risk areas must be avoided. In the Christian life, discipline is essential. It can never be displaced by liberty.

A young Christian friend made a wise observation that touches upon the truth of this passage. "Some Christians are not strong enough to expose themselves to certain temptations," he said. Then after naming some specific areas he continued, "They are still trying to break old habits. They will never be able to overcome those habits unless they stay away from all that temptation."

His conclusion is the same as that found in 1 Corinthians 10:14—flee!

The intent of the passage seems to be more than a warning against falling into temptation. The real warning is to stay away from places that expose one to strong temptation. This is a very personal principle in that it speaks to each of us as individuals. I may have to make choices in my life that others will not make. I may choose to avoid certain permissible activities and places because I find them to be high risk areas for me.

For those who ignored the first two warnings and persisted in their right to consume meat at a heathen religious feast, Paul made one final point.

*Warning #3. Liberty ends where compromise begins.* The apostle's final concern about the heathen religious festival had to do with the question of compromise. He pointed to a definite relationship between the religious feast and fellowship with demons. To demonstrate that he called upon the Corinthians to judge the facts (10:15-21).

Eating at any altar presupposes fellowship with the person of that altar. When Christians took Communion, they fellowshiped with Christ (verse 16). When the Jews ate of the sacrifice from the altar, they fellowshiped with the God of that altar (verse 18). When Gentiles sacrificed to idols, there was fellowship with demons (verse 20).

Such reasoning can lead to but one conclusion. One cannot fellowship with God and with devils. Clearly that would be an attempt at compromise.

For all believers armed with their liberating knowledge Paul made one thing very clear—liberty ends where com-

promise begins. Essentially, he here demanded that believers stay away from heathen feasts.

*Other limitations.* The Corinthians were left with the question, Should a believer ever eat meat offered to idols? After
the warnings, is it possible that there is any kind of situation
in which a Christian may find meat to be both permissible
and good?

Several possible situations were examined. The first was
the question of buying meat in the market. If a Christian
bought meat in the market, some of it most certainly would
be meat that had been offered to idols. Paul's advice was
to buy it, eat it, and ask no questions. It should not be a
matter of concern.

The next situation involved a private dinner party. What
if an unbeliever invites you to dinner where the entree is
apt to be meat that has been offered to idols? Paul concluded that if you want to go, then go. Don't ask questions.
Eat whatever is set before you.

Then, once again he qualified his basic statement. "If
anyone points out that the meat has been offered to idols,
then don't eat it. Abstain for the sake of the conscience of
the speaker. Don't give occasion here for your liberty to
be judged by another man's conscience."

If all this seems contradictory, we need only look at Paul's
concluding remarks on the meat issue. It is not important
what you eat. What is important is that whatever you eat,
or drink, or do, you do it all to glorify God. The believer
who glorifies God is not going to be an offense to others.
He is going to put aside his rights to serve others. Paul's
final challenge is that the believers should follow his example as he followed Christ. Certainly no greater example
could be found. Our Lord set aside His rights and became
as a servant that we might be free from the power and
penalty of sin.

Believers have a continuing responsibility to develop the
ability to make judgments concerning personal Christianity. What is the issue with which you struggle? In judging

what is right or wrong for you, are you distinguishing between that which is permissible and that which is good? Do you keep in mind that liberty, uncontrolled by love, quickly becomes license?

It was never the intent of the apostle to take away a meat eater's liberty. Rather, he urged those believers to impose self-limitations when the occasion called for it. In addressing those ancient questions, he has left with us some abiding principles for making judgments in the twentieth century.

* A believer should never do anything that is permissible if in so doing he becomes a stumbling block to another believer.
* A Christian should avoid places that constitute high risk areas for personal temptation.
* A Christian's liberty always ends where compromise begins.

From the first century to the present, the biblical principles remain the same.

Only the issues have changed.

# DIVISION IV

# MAKING JUDGMENTS: DISCERNMENT

Developing the ability to make judgments should be an on-going process for the believer. Critical evaluation is good. Discernment is better.

In making critical evaluations, the believer is called upon to weigh facts and balance principles in order to make a decision. He may be confronted with those facts in a variety of ways. Once he sees them he makes a judgment on the situation.

In practicing discernment, the believer goes a step further. He sizes up the situation for himself. He is able to recognize all the implications of a given situation and then act in an appropriate manner. By contrast, failing to practice discernment often results in inappropriate behavior.

Several Greek words are translated "discernment," but *diakrino* is the one that best indicates acutely developed judgment. It is from this word that we gain our English word *diacritical*. Diacritical markings are those markings found in the dictionary to indicate how a letter is to be pronounced, for example, ä ā ȧ. *Diakrino* denotes making judgments that involve the recognition of subtle differences.

Although much like critical evaluation, discernment implies more expertise. It is the ultimate of personal judgment. It is the judgment of the mature.

Paul decried the lack of discernment evidenced in the lives of the Corinthian believers. Likewise, the writer to the Hebrews spoke of this lack in the lives of the Jewish Christians to whom he wrote. In each letter the unmistakable emphasis concerning discernment is that it presupposes maturity.

In the following section we will examine the relationship between maturity and discernment. We will suggest ways to develop discernment. We will demonstrate how the observance of Communion demands continuing discernment on the part of participants. And, finally, we will show the relationship between love and discernment.

# 11

## The Relationship Between Maturity and Discernment

There is an old folk story about a little boy who, in the name of obedience, carried melting butter in his cap, wrapped a kitten in wet banana leaves, and tied a loaf of bread to a string and dragged it home behind him. In a final display of "obedience" he stepped very carefully right in the middle of thirteen freshly baked pies.

This little boy tried very hard to do exactly what his mother said but had virtually no understanding of what she meant. Somehow I always think of his story in connection with immaturity among believers.

Some Christians can be very zealous and very intent on obeying the Lord, yet be totally lacking in discernment. Such believers have no personal ability to analyze a situation and then apply correct principles.

Discernment is an acquired skill. About that there can be little doubt. Children are not expected to show acuteness of judgment. It is assumed that acquiring discernment is part of the growing-up process. The adolescent who gives evidence of discernment is characterized as one who is very mature for his or her age. Discernment is generally acknowledged as the judgment of the mature.

*Spiritual maturity and spiritual discernment.* Spiritual discernment accompanies spiritual maturity. The two cannot be separated. Where immaturity is evident, discernment will be lacking.

The unnamed writer of the book of Hebrews provides us with an important perspective on discernment (5:11-14). Particularly, he shows the relationship between discernment and maturity.

There were many things the writer wished to convey to those Jewish believers concerning Christ, the great High Priest. But it was hard to communicate the truths because the recipients of the letter were so slow to learn.

The writer pointedly reminded them that at this stage of their Christian lives they should have been teaching others. Instead, it was necessary for them to be taught all over again the rudiments of the faith.

These rudiments are compared to milk, the diet of babies. In contrast, strong meat is the diet of mature people.

The implication of this passage is that in a normal growth pattern, maturity will be evidenced by an ability to discern. This is not accomplished through the mere passing of time. A believer gains discernment as he exercises his senses over a period of time. Failing to so exercise impedes the growth process; consequently the believer is seen to be spiritually underdeveloped.

*The Corinthians lacked maturity and discernment.* Early in his letter to the Corinthians (3:1) Paul refers to their need to progress from the diet of babies to the diet of the mature. He implies that their growth pattern has not developed normally. They are spiritually underdeveloped.

The Corinthians also lacked discernment. They could not discern the work of grace in their own lives. They were oblivious to the fact that whatever they had was a gift from God. They had no understanding of the significance of the

Lord's Table. Their lack of discernment was identified as the source of God's judgment upon them. This passage, 11:17-34, will be discussed in the next chapter.

Over the years we have discovered that the "Corinthian combination" can be devastating to a church. Wherever there is zeal, knowledge, and spiritual gifts coupled with a lack of discernment, there is potential for great problems.

Certainly we do not wish to discourage zeal, knowledge, or the proper exercise of gifts. These are harbingers of new life in the church. But unless that combination is tempered by discernment, the new life can quickly become a very troubled existence.

It becomes the task of the leadership (clergy and lay) to develop maturity within the body. Only as maturity is developed will discernment come.

*Developing maturity.* How did Paul attempt to correct the Corinthian problem? In addition to demanding obedience to the revealed Word of God, he encouraged believers to think, to reason, and to discern.

In reading his writings to the early churches one begins to wonder if it would not have been easier to send those Christians more specific codes of conduct. "These are your dos and don'ts. By following them you will always know exactly how a Christian should conduct himself." Especially would this seem desirable for the spiritually immature Corinthians. But of course Paul never did that.

Under the guidance of the Holy Spirit he taught first-century believers that Christianity is for thinkers. To exercise one's faith properly one should learn to weigh facts, apply principles, test all things, and make distinctions that involve very subtle differences.

Although he consistently refused to lay down a new law, Paul constantly held before the believers a new standard of living. He challenged Christians to be a separated people. On this he was adamant. He was just as adamant about personal responsibility in discerning what is right and proper behavior.

If we would follow his methods we must teach new believers to obey, to think, to reason, and to discern.

*Discipleship, a key to maturity.* Discipleship is a major key to Christian maturity. Admittedly we may be less than objective here, since our ministry has been redirected into one that is almost exclusively one of discipling. But it has been our experience over the past decade that a novice matures best as he enters into a personal discipleship program.

In a discipleship program the novice learns through interaction, through correction, through specific direction, and through personal encouragement. The goal of the discipleship program is maturity as evidenced by an ever-increasing ability to exercise discernment.

Contrary to what some may advocate, the needs of a novice are not best served through an unstructured group Bible study in which participants are encouraged to express personal opinions on the correct application of a designated Scripture.

At this stage of his life, the novice has more questions than answers. He should be encouraged to concentrate on those questions rather than to express uneducated guesses regarding scriptural application. Certainly this may be accomplished through a group Bible study as well as a one-on-one study; however it must be a carefully directed study in which the leader assumes responsibility for correcting the statements of the participants.

In his study, as in his life, the novice progresses best when he makes himself accountable to a mature leader.

It is a good biblical principle that a novice should take correction during the process of learning. That means being accountable. It means submitting to mature leaders. Paul demanded submission to himself. He also demanded that the believers submit to Timothy and to other spiritual leaders. And, of course, he always demanded submission to God's revealed directives.

*The care and feeding of a novice: a case history.* Several years ago, we watched the growth process in a certain new believer. With all the fervor of a first-century zealot, Tim entered into his new life. A lay leader began to disciple him. Week after week he poured his life into Tim's, kept Tim accountable, encouraged him when he failed, and in general tried to answer the endless questions that arose out of Tim's daily Bible reading.

Even with all that discipling, Tim created some problems. Every week he found some new concept that he quickly turned into a direct command. While his zeal was commendable, his lack of discernment often kept him at odds with the established church—there were too many Cadillacs in the congregation. And too many diamond earrings. And, for that matter, too many washing machines. Christians should not spend their money on such things. Of course Tim had to be told that by using his mother-in-law's washing machine he was weakening his argument considerably.

In spite of problems, Tim's zeal also brought blessings. It was through his simplistic approach to Scripture that a new ministry was started by the church.

One day Tim's mentor called. "Pastor, I have a question. Tim wants to know what Matthew twenty-five, thirty-six means. You know that's the verse that says, 'I was in prison and you came to me.' I told him I guess it means we're supposed to visit those in prison. So then he asked me, 'When do we go? I was in every jail in this county, and no one ever came to see me.' I didn't know how to answer that, but I told him that I would call Pastor Gage to see what could be done."

Obviously it proved to be the Lord's timing. Pastor Gage immediately called the jail, and permission was granted to visit the prisoners on a weekly basis. (It had been refused on a previous occasion.) During the next several years over 100 decisions a year were recorded in that jail. The ministry also proved to be a training ground for Tim, who went weekly to tell what God was doing in his life.

(Throughout Tim's growth period, we often discussed his progress and lack of progress. Ken was much more optimistic than I. I tended to be exasperated each time Tim's latest tangent surfaced. But Ken said on more than one occasion, "Tim is bright, and he is in the Word continually. In time he will gain more discernment." And of course he did.—Joy)

*Dangers accompanying lack of discernment.* Lack of discernment is a common characteristic of the immature Christian. Because he does not exercise discernment, the immature believer is in a vulnerable position. He is easily deceived and is open to deviation of doctrine.

First Timothy 3:6-7 gives weight to this thought. The context concerns qualifications for an overseer in the church. Along with some very stringent qualifications about his personal and family life is the stipulation that the overseer not be a novice. As such, he would be vulnerable to pride and to deception by Satan. Verse 7 indicates that the overseer should also have had time to establish a good reputation as a Christian. There should be no remaining problem from former life-styles in a man who is being considered for the office of an overseer.

As lay people, it was once our experience to walk into a new church in a new town where a novice had just been called as the pastor. The man had been a Christian for less than six months, was still trying to break old habits, and had less Bible knowledge than any adult member of his congregation.

Implausible as this may sound, it happened in a conservative, evangelical church. The small congregation grew tired of waiting for God's man (or God's time) and concluded that an unqualified pastor was better than no pastor at all.

Of course it did not work. Discouraged over lack of training and an inability to exercise judgment, the novice soon resigned.

A much more common problem is the situation in which

church leaders (clergy and lay) insist upon putting a new believer in a place of responsibility within the church. They defend this practice by pointing to the obvious shortage of workers. Often they reason that the new believer should be given a place of responsibility "to encourage him." There is no biblical basis for such rationale. This is not to say, of course, that maturity is a qualification for every job in the church.

It is hard to be objective about the novice who is openly enthusiastic. It is easy to allow all that zeal to become the overriding qualification for some position of responsibility. But caution should be exercised when the job is one that carries responsibility for the spiritual welfare of the body. For this area, one needs the spiritual discernment of a mature believer.

*There is no substitute for maturity.* The negative example of the Corinthians should be a clear warning to all Christians that there is no substitute for maturity.

Knowledge is not a substitute.

Zeal is not a substitute.

The possession of spiritual gifts is not a substitute. As has been noted several times, the Corinthians had all these qualifications. Yet Paul labeled them a carnal church and reproved them for their immaturity.

If we would seek discernment for our churches, then it is essential to encourage the development of Christian maturity, for which there is no substitute and apart from which there is little real discernment.

# 12

## Love, Discernment, and the Lord's Supper
### (1 Corinthians 11:17-34)

The Lord's Supper is one of those issues on which Christendom has differed for centuries. How shall it be observed? When shall it be observed? How often? Who should partake? What should the elements be? Does it convey grace or is it a memorial?

Should it be the first Sunday or the last? Once a month or once a year? Shall we serve wine or grape juice? Bread or unleavened wafers? Should participants be served in their seats or come to the altar rail? Should all members be served? All believers? Or all in attendance?

There remains but one question to consider. When the body partakes of the Lord's Supper, is it beneficial or detrimental?

With scathing denunciations and specific accusations, Paul communicated to the Corinthian church that their observance of the Lord's Table was not to their good. Their total lack of discernment rendered the ordinance more detrimental than beneficial.

This lack of discernment, evidenced by highly inappropriate behavior, made a mockery of the ordinance and incurred judgment upon the participants.

*When is the Lord's Supper not the Lord's Supper?* Although the Corinthians faithfully kept the ordinance, Paul refused to commend them for it. He denounced their ever-present division, which followed them even to the Communion table.

To the feast that preceded the actual Communion the rich brought great quantities of food, which they consumed while the poor went hungry. Compounding the problem was their practice of excessive drinking and approaching the Communion table in a state of intoxication.

This despicable behavior prompted Paul to rehearse once again the historical significance of the ordinance. The purpose of the Lord's Supper was to demonstrate through a ritual that Christ gave His body and shed His blood for the sins of the world. In effect, the participants were to act out a sermon even as they partook of the elements.

Instead of acting out a sermon, however, the Corinthians acted out their divisions. Instead of preaching Christ's death, they polarized Christ's church.

Whatever else the Corinthian celebration might have been called, Paul declared that it certainly was not the Lord's Supper.

*When does the Communion table become a place of judgment?* For the Corinthians, the Communion table became a place of judgment when their lack of discernment caused them to approach the table in an unworthy manner. Divine judgment brought illness and even death to some of the participants.

In a sense, Paul's solution suggests that the Communion table should always be a place of personal judgment. "Judge or be judged" is his admonition. "If we would judge ourselves we would not be judged."

Self-judgment has two parts. Examine and eat. The passage implies that there is danger in eating without exam-

ining. But it assumes that the self-examination is to be
followed by eating. It should never be assumed that one
might examine oneself with the idea of abstaining.

At the Communion table the believer is to pause, to
examine his own heart, and deal with his attitude. The
purpose is to insure against approaching the table in an
unworthy manner.

*The relationship of love and the Communion table.* It is significant that Paul concluded the instructions concerning
the Lord's Supper by admonishing the believers once again
to show love and respect for one another. Until their divisions were healed they could not observe the ordinance
properly.

The Corinthian experience at the Lord's Supper vividly
illustrates the relationship between love, discernment, and
the Communion table. If the Corinthians had possessed
any discernment regarding the ordinance, they would have
known that division had no place at the table. They would
have understood that in order to show forth the Lord's
death one must also show love for the Lord's people.

It is impossible to observe the Lord's Supper while dis-
daining the Lord's people. The same Lord who said, "Do
this in remembrance of Me," commanded His followers to
love one another.

When a believer truly discerns the significance of this
ordinance he will see the need to learn to love fellow believers. It is in the periodic observation of the age-old ritual
that Christians should be reminded to put aside differences, heal breaches, and reach out in love to fellow Christians. It is here that the body is healed.

What value does the ritual have when observed amidst
division where hostility hangs in the very air? What significance would the ordinance have? Where there is neither
discernment, nor self-judgment, nor healing of the body,
a meaningful ritual is reduced to a perfunctory exercise.

*Encouraging love at the Lord's Supper.* Any call to demonstrate love within the body is apt to elicit a certain

amount of honest skepticism today. The Christian church has recently come through an era in which superficial love and contrived fellowship became the focus of our faith. Instant intimacy was the goal. It sounded good, but overall it produced very little genuine caring.

Logistics alone tell us that one cannot be best friends with everyone in the church. There is not time to develop and nurture that many real friendships. But we have a responsibility to show love and communicate care for one another.

In our experience the Communion table has served as a practical reminder of this responsibility. It has been the occasion for some very meaningful expressions of love within the body.

Specifically, here are some moments that have made the observance of the ordinance special. Most are part of the ritual. One is spontaneous. All have served to remind us of love within the body.

• The quiet time allowed for self-examination prior to partaking of the elements. It is hard to meditate on God's love without confessing ill feelings harbored in the heart.

• That time in which the deacons and pastor serve each other. In full view of the congregation, the seated deacons are served by the pastor. In turn he seats himself and is then served by one of the deacons. This unhurried demonstration of serving one another is a picture of what our relationship should be within the body.

• The conclusion. Joining hands and circling the sanctuary after the ordinance is an effective reminder of the oneness (or need for oneness) within the body.

• A spontaneous moment. A deacon in one of our congregations is responsible for one of the most meaningful spontaneous moments of our experience. He was standing alongside his fellow deacons at the Communion table just prior to serving the participants. Quietly he asked for permission to speak. Permission granted, he tearfully offered a public apology for harsh words he had spoken to some of the people. His action demonstrated his deep discernment of the occasion.

*Responsibility of pastor and people concerning the Lord's Supper.* Keeping before the congregation the meaning of the ritual is the continuing responsibility of the pastor. In addition there are times when it becomes necessary for a pastor to remind the body that true discernment of the occasion demands the healing of divisions that may exist within the body.

Individually, it is the believer's responsibility to deal with attitudes that need correction. Making a concentrated effort to see others as God sees them is a positive approach to dealing with negative feelings. It helps to remember that your fellow believer is also the object of God's love. He too has received God's grace. He also possesses spiritual gifts, and he, along with you, is an heir of God.

One thing that should come from the continued observance of the Communion table is a deeper love for one another. If that fails to happen, it is indicative of a lack of discernment of the true significance of the ordinance.

Paul's desire for the Corinthians was that they should put away the divisions that fractured their body. He opened his first letter to them with this plea. He closed his last letter to them with the same plea.

His letters reveal the relationship between their divisions and problems with judging. By judging all the wrong things they divided the church. By failing to judge sin within the body they corrupted the church. By failing to judge personal sin they weakened the church.

These are all corporate problems. But they begin in the heart of the individual. It is there that they must be solved. What better place to begin than at the Communion table?

Ecclesiastical powers will continue to determine how and when the ordinance will be observed. But only the individual can determine if it is to be beneficial or detrimental.

Moody Press, a ministry of the Moody Bible Institute, is designed for education, evangelization, and edification. If we may assist you in knowing more about Christ and the Christian life, please write us without obligation: Moody Press, c/o MLM, Chicago, IL 60610.

# Corinth Reexamined

The church at Corinth has always been seen as a negative example—disunity, lack of spiritual judgment, and carnality all characterized this church. Who would seek to pattern a church after this first-century example?

A close examination of Paul's greeting to the Corinthian believers reveals that the church at Corinth actually had some positive characteristics. They were, in fact, born-again believers who were boldly witnessing of their faith and looking for the Lord's return. That is not to say that they were a spiritual church. It is just to point out that in looking at the complete picture of the Corinthian body we discover a warning for the church today.

Negative problems that characterized the Corinthian church can and do exist in churches that exude positive characteristics. But the negative overshadowed the positive.

Whatever else a church has going for it, if disunity and lack of spiritual judgment abound it is a carnal church.